English Kings Killing Foreigners

Nina Bowers and Philip Arditti

T0027180

methuen | drama

LONDON • NEW YORK • OXFORD • NEW DELHI • SYDNEY

METHUEN DRAMA
Bloomsbury Publishing Plc
50 Bedford Square, London, WC1B 3DP, UK
1385 Broadway, New York, NY 10018, USA
29 Earlsfort Terrace, Dublin 2, Ireland

BLOOMSBURY, METHUEN DRAMA and the Methuen
Drama logo are trademarks of Bloomsbury Publishing Plc

First published in Great Britain 2024

Cover design by William Andrews

Cover photo by Zbigniew Kotkiewicz

A catalogue record for this book is available from the British Library.

Library of Congress Control Number: 2024935312

ISBN: PB: 978-1-3505-1085-2
ePDF: 978-1-3505-1086-9
eBook: 978-1-3505-1087-6

Series: Modern Plays

Typeset by Mark Heslington Ltd, Scarborough, North Yorkshire

To find out more about our authors and books visit
www.bloomsbury.com and sign up for our newsletters.

Realfake Theatre and Camden People's Theatre presents

English Kings Killing Foreigners

By Nina Bowers and Philip Arditti

English Kings Killing Foreigners is commissioned and co-produced by Camden People's Theatre and supported by the National Lottery Project Grants via the Arts Council England and the Paul Hamlyn Foundation.

English Kings Killing Foreigners was first performed at the Camden People's Theatre on Tuesday 23 April 2024.

English Kings Killing Foreigners

By Nina Bowers and Philip Arditti

Performer and Director	Philip Arditti
Performer and Director	Nina Bowers
Co-director	Milli Bhatia
Producer	María Cuervo
Set and Costume Designer	Erin Guan
Sound Designer	Jamie Lu
Lighting Designer	Jodie Underwood
Production Manager	Agustín Masondo
Technical Stage Manager	Jim Spencer Broadbent
Creative Collaborator	Hannah Ringham

Philip Arditti

Philip Arditti is a London-based actor, writer and theatre-maker from Turkey.

Writing includes: *Extinct* (Winner of Global Jewish Voices Award, published by Methuen as part of Global Jewish Plays); *Knock Knock* (*Burnt at the Stake*, an evening of new writing at the Shakespeare's Globe); co-writer and director of Turkey-Syria Fundraiser at the Royal Albert Hall.

Translations into Turkish include: *The Father, Tape* and *Facts*.

His theatre acting credits include: *Baghdaddy, Who Cares, Living Newspaper* (Royal Court Bath); *Copenhagen* (Theatre Royal Bath); *Henry IV Parts 1 and 2, Henry V, Henry VI, Parts 1, 2 and 3, Richard III* (Shakespeare's Globe); *Oslo, Salome, As You Like It, The Holy Rosenbergs, Blood and Gifts, England People Very Nice* (National Theatre); *The Hunting Lodge, The Fourth Wise Man* (Unicorn Theatre); *Henry V* (Regent's Park Open Air Theatre); *Catch 22* (UK tour); Light *Shining in Buckinghamshire, A Family Affair, Silver Birch House* (Arcola Theatre).

TV and film acting credits include: *Breathtaking, Day of the Jackal, Protection, No Return, Domina, Black Earth Rising, Foreign Skies, Sanctuary, Patrick Melrose, The State, L'Ispettore Coliandro, The White Princess, Spotless, Ripper Street, The Honourable Woman, Game of Thrones, Strike Back 4, Da Vinci's Demons, Borgia, Son, New Tricks, Twenty Twelve, Accused, Five Days, Father and Son, 10 Days to War, House of Saddam.*

He was part of the founding of the Arcola Theatre where he was an Associate Producer from 2001 to 2007. He was part of the founding of MENA Arts UK where he is still on the steering committee

Nina Bowers

Nina Bowers is an actor, theatre maker and writer.

Acting credits include: *As You Like It* (Shakespeare's Globe); *Girl on an Altar* (Kiln); *Dear Elizabeth* (The Gate); *The Magic Flute* (Complicité); *Henry IV, parts 1 and 2, Henry V, Henry VI* and *Richard III* (Shakespeare's Globe); *The Wolves* (Theatre Royal Stratford East); *Crave* (The Barbican); *Twilight Los Angeles 1992* (The Gate);

Tomorrow I'll be Twenty (Complicité tour); *Screen*: *The Diplomat* (Netflix); *Lockwood and Co* (Netflix).

Writing/making/cabaret: *Ballroom Play* (Theatr Genedlaethol Cymru); co-director of *Letters* (Gate); *An Inconvenient Feeling* (The Yard/ICA). She has performed two original solo works at Camden People's Theatre's Sprint Festival: *Nina Talks About her Values* and *The Mantis from Atlantis*. Nina was nominated by the Globe for the Evening Standard Future Theatre Fund Award in 2021. Nina performs professionally as a drag king and go-go dancer called Sonny Delight and has performed at The Divine, The Glory, the National Theatre, Dalston Superstore, among others. Nina co-devised the family-friendly drag show *On Air* for Bristol Fringe in 2023 and is a Man Up 2022 finalist.

Milli Bhatia

Milli (she/her) is a theatre, film and radio director, and dramaturg from East London. She is an associate artist at Synergy.

She was associate director at the Royal Court, associate artist at the Bush Theatre, resident assistant director at Birmingham Rep and creative associate at the Gate Theatre. Her training includes the National Theatre Director's Programme and The Old Vic 12.

She is a two-time Olivier Award nominee for her productions of *seven methods of killing kylie jenner* and *Blue Mist*, both premiered at the Royal Court Theatre.

Her work as director includes: *Blue Mist* by Mohamed-Zain Dada (Royal Court); *seven methods of killing kylie jenner* by Jasmine Lee-Jones (Jerwood Theatre Upstairs 2019, Jerwood Theatre Downstairs 2021, Film 2022, Public Theater New York and Woolly Mammoth Washington DC 2023, Royal Court); *seven methods of killing kylie jenner* (Swedish language production, Riksteatern, Swedish National Theatre, national tour 2022. Selected to return for the Biennale, Dramaten in 2023); *Chasing Hares* by Sonali Bhattacharyya (Young Vic); *Maryland* by Lucy Kirkwood (co director, Royal Court/South Bank Centre); *My White Best Friend (and Other Letters Left Unsaid)* (Bunker 2018/2019, Royal Court 2020); *Dismantle This Room* by Nina Segal (Bush Theatre/transferred to Royal Court); *Baghdaddy* by Jasmine Naziha Jones (Royal Court); *This Liquid Earth* by Amy Jephta (Royal Court/Edinburgh International Festival); *Home(body)* by Jasmine Lee-Jones (Young Vic); *Yash Gill's Power Half*

Hour by Nikesh Shukla, *The Hijabi Monologues* (Bush Theatre); *Living Newspaper* (Royal Court); *Ghosts in the Blood* by Joel Tan (Audible).

María Cuervo

María Cuervo is a Colombian award-winning multidisciplinary producer. With an MA with Distinction in Creative Producing at the Royal Central School of Speech and Drama, María is highly experienced in producing small and mid-scale theatre, tours and immersive and multidisciplinary performances.

In recent years, she has worked with recognised theatre venues and companies like the Young Vic, LIFT Festival, Theatre Peckham, Certain Blacks, Upswing Aerial, Maya Productions, REcreate Agency, Orange Skies Theatre and Creative Vortex.

Previous producing work includes the 5-star endurance performance *The Second Woman* starring Ruth Wilson (Young Vic and LIFT Festival 2023); *I Love You, Now What?* (The Pleasance and Edinburgh Fringe 2023); *Súper Chefs* (tour 2023); *1797: The Mariner's Revenge* (Old Royal Naval College 2022); *Kelab Malam* (Rich Mix 2021); *Distrito Blair 360* – inspired by George Orwell's *1984* (Sala C 2021); *Trojana Webcamming Chronicles* (Voila! Theatre Festival 2020); *The Apologists* (VAULT Festival 2019); *Balthazar Treasure: The Cacao Quest* (LIFT Festival 2019); *Guerrillera* (Bush Theatre 2019).

Collaborative, resourceful and creative. Interested in multidisciplinary and thought-provoking work. From circus to immersive theatre and multimedia performances, María is passionate about producing work made by underrepresented voices and creatives. Pushing the boundaries between performance and audiences, she loves creating remarkable experiences for audiences and artists alike.

Erin Guan

Erin Guan is a London-based scenographer and interactive installation artist from China. She has a strong interest in interdisciplinary theatre and performance making and she works across installations, plays, musicals, dance, digital theatre, devised theatre. Her work spans intercultural performances and minority voices. Her digital artwork specialises in Augmented Reality and Virtual Reality experiences. Her VR installation Chamber404 is exhibited in Ars Electronica 2020 x Interactive Architecture Lab, Camden People's Theatre and VA Lab

Taipei and Peckham Digital 2023. Her recent theatre projects include: *Romeo and Juliet* (Polka Theatre); *Turandot* (The Opera Makers and Ellandar x Arcola Theatre); *Pied Piper* (Battersea Arts Centre); *The Apology* (New Earth Theatre x Arcola Theatre); *A Gig for Ghost* (Forty Five North x Soho Theatre Upstairs); school touring *Pressure Drop* (Immediate Theatre); immersive technology promenade performance *Unchain Me* (Dreamthinkspeak x Brighton Festival); *Prayer for the Hungry Ghost* (Barbican Open Lab); *Symbiont* (Caged Bird Theatre x The VAULT); *Foxes* (Defibrillator Theatre x Theatre503); touring musical *Tokyo Rose* (Burnt Lemon Theatre); both immersive game theatre *Talk* and *The House Never Wins* (Kill The Cat Theatre); and web design for audio tour *The Letters Project* (Gate Theatre). Her recent TV work includes: costume design for East Mode S2 with Nigel Ng (Comedy Central x Channel 5).

Jamie Lu

Jamie is a London-based scenographer, an award nominated sound designer. Jamie's theatre credits as sound designer include: *Spin* (Hope Theatre/EdFringe23/Arcola Theatre); *Ada* (National Youth Theatre); *Tiger* (Omnibus Theatre); *Shakespeare's RandJ*, *Hedda Gabler* (Reading Rep); *Gentlemen*, *The Apology*, *We Started to Sing*, *Broken Lad* (Arcola Theatre); *Sorry We Didn't Die at Sea* (Park Theatre/Seven Dials Playhouse); *Youth in Asia* (Theatre503); *1984* (London Youth Theatre); *Declan* (Camden People's Theatre/Edinburge Fringe 2023); *Going for Gold*, *Road* (Chelsea Theatre); *Mother's Day*, *Grills*, *Declan* (Camden People's Theatre); *Burnout* (RandD, VAULT Festival and tour); *Still Here* (Jack Studio Theatre); *Smoke*, *Tokyo Rose* (Southwark Playhouse); *Iphigenia* (Hope Theatre); *Fester* (Bridge House Theatre); *A Gig for Ghosts* (Soho Theatre); *Paradise Lost* (Shipwright); *The Unicorn*, *What The Heart Wants*, *How to Build a Wax Figure* (Edinburgh Fringe 2022); *The Blue House* (Blue Elephant Theatre); *Dirty Hearts* (Old Red Lion Theatre). As assistant sound designer: *Henry V* (Donmar Warehouse). Sound design for Audioplay: *The Dream Machine* (Fizzy Sherbet).

Jodie Underwood

Jodie Underwood is a lighting designer with work spanning theatre, opera and dance. She graduated from RADA in 2021 with first class honours and is particularly interested in new writing and more unconventional theatrical forms.

Their recent credits include: *Jab The Play* (Finborough Theatre); *Ruckus* (associate to Simeon Miller, UK tour); *A Christmas Carol* (Taunton Brewhouse); *Cheeky Little Brown* (UK tour); *The Book of Will* (associate to Simeon Miller, Shakespeare North Playhouse); *The Life Sporadic of Jess Wildgoose* (Pleasance, Islington and Pleasance Courtyard, Edinburgh); *Ride* (associate to Jamie Platt, Leicester Curve and Southwark Playhouse); *Pigs Might Fly* (associate to Aaron Dootson, Theatre Peckham); *When Darkness Falls* (Associate to Bethany Gupwell – UK tour); *DNA* (Tara Theatre); *After the Act* (New Diorama Theatre and Traverse, Edinburgh); *Blow Down* (Theatre Royal Wakefield and Leeds Playhouse); *The Boys Are Kissing* (Theatre503); and *Horse-Play* (Riverside Studios).

Agustín "Goose" Masondo

Agustín "Goose" Masondo (he/him) is an Argentina-born London-raised production manager and stage manager. Credits as production manager include: *The Canterbury Tales* (Halfcut Theatre). Credits as stage manager include: *Evelyn* (Southwark Playhouse, Mercury Theatre Colchester); *Another America* (Park Theatre); *Sex Education Xplorers (S.E.X.)* (Summerhall); *The Making of Pinocchio* (Tramway).

Jim Spencer Broadbent

Jim Spencer Broadbent is a freelance stage manager specialising in Fringe Theatre based in south east London. His recent and most noteworthy credits include: the King's Head Theatre in Islington, Above the Stag @ Wonderville and the McEwan Hall in Edinburgh.

Hannah Ringham

Hannah is a writer/performer interested in community and collaboration.

Co-founder of award-winning theatre collective SHUNT, Hannah has performed and co-devised all SHUNT shows and projects including: *The Boy Who Climbed Out of his Face*, *Tropicana* and *Dance Bear Dance* with the Royal National Theatre and the SHUNT Lounge community arts platform project.

Awards for SHUNT work include: the Peter Brook Empty Space Award, the Time Out Live Award and the Total Theatre Award.

Independent work includes: *The Untethered Joke* with Sue MacLaine (DISRUPT Festival, CPT); *Hannah Ringham's Free Show* (*Bring Money*) (British Council Showcase); *I Want Love* (Birmingham Rep); *The Present* (Unicorn Theatre) and *Wedding* with Glen Neath (Shoreditch Town Hall). Hannah received an Arts in Mind award from King's College London for *Die or Run* a comedy performance and discussion piece on mental health and political thinking developed for a diverse audience of postgraduate psychiatry students, mental health service users and the local community. Hannah also recently received an Arts Council of England DYCP (Develop Your Creative Practice) research fund for strategies for new work in theatre and community in their practice. As an performer and artistic collaborator Hannah continues to collaborate with diverse artists such as large scale immersive company Block 9, the poet Jemina Foxtrot and contemporary artists Adam Bloomberg and Olivier Chanerin.

As a performer, Hannah's recent credits/collaborations include: *As You Like It* (The Globe, 2023); *Zoombird* by Caroline Horton (Coventry City of Culture, 2022); *The Mysteries* (Manchester Royal Exchange); *The Unknown Island* with Ellen McDougall (The Gate) and *England* a two-hander award winning play by Tim Crouch which toured internationally to New York, the Melbourne Arts Festival and the Hong Kong Festival among others, and performance interaction projects with BrickBox, Without Walls. Recent radio plays include *Ropewalk House* by Anita Sullivan and *Daphne and Apollo* by Caroline Horton, both for Radio 4.

Current projects in development include: *Take It or Leave It*, a comedy street performance on death, care and protest performed in front of a theatre, developed from a recent MFA project research.

Teaching involves working with numerous arts organisations and institutions including; the Royal Central School of Speech and Drama, Guildhall, Drama Studio and Rose Bruford. Hannah has given many workshops on theatre and performance nationally and internationally as part of touring shows and within the capacity of performance and art related activities.

Other work includes working with many diverse community groups within live art platforms, for example: BAC Youth Theatre, the Black Elders group, Roundhouse Youth Theatre, An Oxford Playhouse Plays Out Commission for care homes within Oxfordshire, Thamesmead Cultural Program. Hannah has also worked as a reader for stroke patients in hospitals and care homes with the charity INTERACT since 2008.

Education and research qualifications: BA (Hons) Brighton University. MFA in Advanced Theatre Practice at the Royal Central School of Speech and Drama. BSL level 1.

Realfake Theatre

Realfake Theatre is a new performance duo by Nina Bowers and Philip Arditti.

Our work is informed by our trained disciplines in classical acting, collaborative and physical theatre. We challenge the classical canon, embrace the making and unmaking of narratives and subvert ideas of autobiography. We collide the personal and political using clown work, multimedia, audience interaction, and autofiction.

Special friends of Realfake Theatre without whose support *English Kings Killing Foreigners* could not have happened: Albert Benbasat, Rina and Michael Citron, Apo Tercanli, Selen and Celal Akata and Nadia and Ralf Arditti.

CAMDEN PEOPLE'S THEATRE

Camden People's Theatre is one of the UK's most influential small theatres, with a proud record of supporting early-career performance makers – to make amazing work, and to establish sustainable careers. It brings together artists and everyone else to connect, imagine, be heard and be entertained. It makes space for the theatre of tomorrow, it celebrates community and it strives to create a more equitable and caring world through extraordinary performance made by and for a wide range of people.

Over thirty years, CPT has fulfilled a national leadership role in the field of innovative contemporary performance. We deliver a wide-ranging programme that champions the next generation of theatre-makers, working with and launching the careers of ground-breaking artists including: Fevered Sleep, Chris Thorpe, Emily Lim (who now runs the National Theatre's Public Acts programme); Scottee, Common Wealth and Nouveau Riche (*Queens of Sheba; For Black Boys . . .*) among many, many others. We have an excellent reputation for supporting early-career artists in this field, and for attracting a consistently young and diverse audience.

Our programme foregrounds performance that addresses issues that matter to people right now and features regular themed festivals tackling socio-political issues affecting our wider community. Since 1997, CPT has programmed the annual Sprint Festival, London's best-established festival of new and unusual theatre, and since 2013 Calm Down, Dear, the UK's first and only festival of innovative feminist theatre. For the last thirteen years, we have also run the unique artist support/peer network programme Starting Blocks, whose alumni include Haley McGee (*Age is a Feeling*); Rachel Mars and piss/carnation.

CPT runs a range of other artist support and project development schemes, designed to support the development of artists and their projects from early ideas through to full-length runs. *English Kings Killing Foreigners* is an excellent example – having received one of our annual seed commissions targeted to artists from marginalised backgrounds, it went on to receive our Home Run commission, which supports projects from work-in-progress stage through to full production for a three-week run in our studio. Home Run offers a substantial cash commission, rehearsal space and co-producing support from CPT to facilitate the development process. Previous

Home Run commissions include *BULLISH* by Milk Presents, *So Many Reasons* by Racheal Ofori and *The Elephant in the Room* by Lanre Malaolu. CPT also founded and chairs the STAMP network of London venues dedicated to artist support, which now numbers more than twenty-five members and facilitates communication between theatre organisations and independent artists. We are also a proud member of our Camden community, and – among many other activities undertaken with local residents – have since 2016 co-run Camden Youth Theatre in collaboration with New Diorama Theatre.

CPT is excited to have supported the development to full production of *English Kings Killing Foreigners*. It's a brilliant example of the bold, unexpected entertaining work we exist to champion. If you'd like to see more of it, and connect today with the performance superstars of tomorrow, come see a show and say hello. You'd be very welcome.

Staff List

Co-Chief Executives: Kaya Stanley-Money and Brian Logan
Artistic Director: Brian Logan
Executive Director: Kaya Stanley-Money
General Manager: Emma Groome
Deputy General Manager: Jeanie Barnsley
Marketing Manager: Kathryn Singleton
Artist Support Producer: Sam Edmunds
Technical Manager: Juliann Pichelski
Duty Technician: Chuck SJ
Front of House Manager: Adam Gregory

Front of House Team

Princess Bestman
Leila Carroll
Atlas Corsini
Sarah Deller
Simone French
Iulia Isar
Heather Jones
Nawel Kobb
Matt Matterson
Art Merluzzi
Becca Millar
Ella Pound
Tilda Shearing

THANKS

PA NB

To Brian Logan and Kaya Stanley-Money.

To Sarah Bedi and Gabi Spiro for giving us a brilliant start.

To Hannah Ringham, Becky Latham, Tim Crouch, Kerry Kyriacos Michael and Lloyd Trott.

To Michelle Terry, Federay Holmes, Sean Holmes and the Globe Ensemble '19 for bringing us together.

To Leyla Nazli, Mehmet Ergen, Laila Alj and Jane Fallowfield.

To Livia Arditti, Serdar Bilis and Seçil Honeywill.

PA

To Mina and Lia.

To Isabella Prigione.

NB

To Kate Nash and Morgan Bowers and Samuel Bowers.

FOREWORD

This play is the result of countless conversations between Phil, Shakespeare, England and I. We met in 2019 while working on the History plays at The Globe. We started having backstage chats, greenroom chats, stage door chats about *Henry V* and why we're still staging it now. Somehow, almost five years on, we are still having those conversations. *English Kings Killing Foreigners* is an attempt to theatricalize the questions, traps and stumbling blocks we've come across along the way.

This play started in the margins of *Henry V* – that most English of plays – by two actors who in different ways are 'outsiders' to Englishness. We connected through that common feeling and made connections between acting, citizenship, rebellion and reform. We were bit-parts in Henry's story and in England's story. Stories that are hard to resist. England, empire and British cultural output (namely Shakespeare) has shaped us politically and personally in countless ways. We choose to work in this industry and in this country because we are able to be 'Ourselves' (whatever that means) in our work. However, there are ghosts here, ghosts of empire, exceptionalism, assimilation. Our existences both on and off the stage slip through these troubling realities, navigating hand-me down narratives while tentatively weaving our own. We hope this play engages the audience in that active journey. We intend it as a mirror held up to the theatre we love; a theatre that is dependent on Shakespeare for survival; a Shakespeare that is tied into Englishness and unavoidably – British notions of cultural supremacy. A strange family. Phil said the other day that Shakespeare is like an unpredictable uncle beloved but also slightly dangerous. We invite him into our evenings hoping for delight, but more often than not, we are faced with discomfort. We love him but we'd probably be better off keeping encounters to a minimum . . . either that or family therapy! Maybe this play is an attempt at the latter.

Nina

PS: At the time of publication we have not yet shared this version of the piece with an audience. We can't wait to see where the conversation goes next. But also this text could differ from what you might see in performance.

English Kings Killing Foreigners

Performance note

This piece was developed through our personal experiences but can be performed by anyone. We encourage the personal stories and biographies to be adapted to anyone wanting to perform this play.

Cast

Nina, *mid twenties, non-gender specific, global majority*
Phil, *mid forties, non-gender specific, global majority*

Act One

Scene One

The game

Preset. The shutters in the theatre are open natural light, work lights in the space, the door to the theatre is open, everything informal.

Phil *and* **Nina** *walk in energetically and open the shutters. They're wearing t-shirts with RealFake Theatre's logo on it. Party music.*

Nina   Hi everyone, my name is Nina.

Phil   Hi, my name is Phil.

Nina   How is everyone doing?

Phil   Brilliant.

Nina   We are the creators of English Kings Killing Foreigners.

Phil   Welcome.

Nina   Let's start with a game.

Nina *writes the following on the back wall:*

. . . .

Kings

. . . .

Foreigners

Nina   Can anyone fill in the blanks?

Audience member does.

Phil   Well done. Round of applause for the winner.

Nina   And now

She writes the following on the back wall:

> . . . .
>
> . . . .
>
> *Killing*
>
> . . . .

Audience fill in the blanks.

Phil Congratulations. Give yourselves a round of applause.

Nina Let's play another game. We'll each audition to play the King. You can vote.

Phil *goes out. Enters as the King.*

Phil I am the king.

Nina *does the same.*

Audience votes and the King is anointed.

Nina And now you can choose how the King will kill the foreigner.

On the back wall **Nina** *writes:*

> *Knife*
>
> *Bow and arrow*
>
> *Gun*

Audience vote. Then **Phil** *and* **Nina** *re-enact the King killing the foreigner.*

They bow.

Nina Great. Is everyone safely settled in? Then let's start the play.

They close the shutters.

Blackout.

Soundscape.

Act Two

Scene One

The meeting

Lights up. **Nina** *by the door. Sunglasses, fake fur, backpack.*

Phil *is further away, well dressed with a satchel and another larger bag.* **Phil** *has a slightly over the top RP accent from now on.*

Nina *really struggling with the locked door, maybe it'll open. She's annoyed at the door, at herself, at the world.*

Nina   FUUUCKKKKKK!

Phil *goes to the door and tries it. He's surprised it's locked.*

Nina (*under her breath*)   Fucking hell! I'm such a fucking idiot!

Phil   What?

Sorry, what did you say?

Nina   Nothing, sorry.

Silence as they consider what to do with this situation.

Phil   So strange.

I mean, it should be open.

Nina   But it's locked.

Shit.

Pause.

Phil   How long have you been here?

Nina   I got here just before you.

Phil   Nobody came by to go in.

Nina   No, otherwise I'd be in. Or they'd be here with me. It's just the two of us.

Phil   Right. Sorry, are you . . . ?

Nina   What?

Phil   Nothing.

Phil *takes out his phone and records a voice message.*

Hi, Victoria. OMG, such a long time. Can't wait to catch up. Listen, I'm just outside the building and I'm a bit late actually and I'm locked out, we're . . . I'm not alone, there's this lady here, sorry, I mean woman, girl, person, lady person.

Nina   Nina.

Phil   Nina! I'm Phil, nice to meet you!

So yeah, Nina and I are waiting here and anyway, be great if you could come down to let me, us, in . . . thank you.

Ends the call.

Stage management will be a couple of minutes.

Nina   Are you rehearsing here?

Phil   Yeah, are you?

Nina   Yeah.

Phil   Oh amazing.

Phil *and* **Nina**   What's the play?

Laughter.

Phil *and* **Nina**   *Henry V.*

And more.

Nina   Oh my god, me too.

Phil   Yeah, you just said.

Nina   Yeah, we said it.

Phil   At the same time. Really?

Nina   Really what?

Phil   You're in Henry with Stuart Dunlop?

Nina   With Stuart, yes!

Phil   Wow. We're gonna do a play together.

Nina   Wow.

Phil   That great English hero's story.

Nina   Who are you playing?

Phil   Have a guess.

Nina   I don't know the play super well.

Phil   It's a biggish one.

Nina   . . . um.

Phil

O, *for* a muse of fire that would ascend
The brightest heaven of invention!
A kingdom for a stage, princes to act,
And monarchs to behold the swelling scene!

Nina   Wow, you're the Chorus?

Phil

Then should the warlike Harry, like himself,
Assume the port of Mars, and at his heels,
Leashed in like hounds, should famine, sword, and fire
Crouch for employment.

Nina   OK yes, you're the Chorus.

Phil

But pardon gentles, the flat unraised spirits
That have dared on this unworthy scaffold
To bring forth so great an object

Nina   Yeah, that's definitely the Chorus.

Phil   Did you catch the stress?

Nina   Do I seem stressed?

Phil   No, I mean the emphasis, like the accent-tuation, the force on the word, the ictus.

Nina   What ictus?

Phil   On *for*.

Nina   Do you mean like someone having a stroke?

Phil   A stroke? Yes, on the word *for*. Lean on it. Most people go for '*O* for a muse of fire', I'm doing '*O for* a muse'. They do *O* for, I'm *O for*. *O* for or *O for*.

Nina   I get it.

Beat.

Phil   Who are you playing?

Nina   Onwards Ho! . . . Soldier number 3.

Phil   No small parts –

Nina   – Only small actors.

Phil   Exactly.

Nina   Yeah, I'm just really here to soak it all in; you know, working with greats like Stuart and Martin . . . and you!

Phil   Oh please, I'm . . . thank you! It's a pleasure to be working with you too.

Nina   Do you have a paracetamol or ibuprofen?

Phil   No, sorry.

They wait. **Phil** *tries the door again.*

Just in case it's suddenly . . .

This could be a health and safety issue. For people inside.

They wait.

Nina   Any news? On the message?

Phil   No.

They wait.

Phil   Nice weather today.

Nina   Yeah, lovely.

Phil   It was so grim yesterday.

Nina   Oh yeah, awful.

Phil   Apparently it's gonna rain next week.

Nina   So shit.

Phil   I know. But they're expecting a heat wave after that.

Nina   Climate change.

Phil   I know, it's so terrible, obviously I'm happy about the sun but it's kind of – A key box!

Nina   What?

Phil   There's a key box, there. Like an airbnb key box!

Nina   OMG!

Phil   That's got to have the key to the building.

Nina   We don't know the code though.

Phil   We could try . . . 2012.

Nina   The end of the world.

Phil   What?! No, the Olympics!

Nina   That's not it. 2023?

Phil   Maybe they haven't gotten around to changing it.

Nina   No. 2022, 21, 20, 19. Why are we just thinking of years?

Phil   1415, the Battle of Agincourt.

Nina   Whoa, you've done your research.

Nina   No. What about something that's not a year?

Phil   1901 William Poel stars and directs *Henry V* to unite the country during the Boar War.

Nina   No.

Phil   1944 Lawrence Olivier stars and directs *Henry V* to unite the country during World War Two.

Nina   No.

Phil   1989 Kenneth Branagh stars and directs *Henry V* post the Falklands War.

Nina   No.

Phil   1993 Stuart Dunlop gets an Olivier for his first portrayal of Henry V during the first Gulf War.

Nina   No.

Phil   FUCK!

Nina   Not sure we're gonna get this, sorry.

Phil   OK OK OK. 1564 birth of William Shakespeare, not just the greatest English playwright ever but the greatest dramatic icon of history.

Nina   YES!

Phil   What?

Nina   Yes! It's open.

Phil   OMG, that's amazing, yes yes yes.

They hug, both really happy.

Nina   There's a key.

Phil   That's it, baby, we're in.

Nina   WE ARE COMING IN, YOU FUCKING
BASTARDS!

Phil *gets his bag.*

Nina   It's not working. FUCK!

Phil   What? Oh for heaven's sake.

Nina   What do we have to do, man! So annoying. Argh! I
wanna get in.

Heeeey! We're out here. Hello. Victoriaaaa! Stuart STUART
DUNLOOOOP.

Phil   Nina, stop please, you can't shout his name in the
middle of the street.

Nina   I HATE EVERYTHING!!! WHY DOES THIS
ALWAYS HAPPEN TO ME! Ugrh and I need a weeeeee.

Nina *has a tantrum.*

Phil   Nina, are you OK!? Enough. It's fine. Let's just sit
down, all right. Look, if you really need to go, I don't mind.
Go for it.

Nina *is taken aback and embarrassed by* **Phil***'s offer.*

Phil   Go on. I'll turn around. English people do it all the
time in the street.

Nina   No, I'm not going to pee in an alleyway outside my
workplace. I can hold it.

They sit.

I went out last night and it was a bit stupid and I got a bit
carried away, was just a bit nervous for today and wanted to
blow off some steam, and I got home at like six and then I
overslept and, yeah . . . now we're stuck here so . . . I just
wanted to make a good impression . . . for once.

Phil   At least you're not alone. Something's gonna happen,
don't worry. Patience.

They wait.

Are you thinking of applying too, for citizenship?

Nina   Oh no, I was born here, I'm British.

Phil   Oh, your accent is . . . ?

Nina   I grew up in Canada.

Phil   Parents?

Nina   My mum's from Essex, my dad's from St Lucia, in the Caribbean.

Have you worked with Stuart before?

Phil   Oh yeah, few times.

Waiting. **Nina** *starts investigating the door as* **Phil** *speaks.*

Phil   I've wanted to play the Chorus for such a long time, this captivating narrator that guides us through the story of the hero in the making. He's like a timer at the top of each act, setting the scene for what's to come. The lens through which we see the hero.

Shakespeare himself is thought to have played him in 1605.

Nina   So you are Shakespeare?

OTT reaction from **Phil**.

Nina   You like that?

Phil   It's not everyday I get compared to Shakespeare.

Nina   I'm not the biggest fan if I'm honest.

Phil   What do you mean?

Nina   I don't know . . . I just never really felt like it was for me.

Phil   The language can be hard to understand but you just have to let it wash over you. He writes for everyone.

Nina   I guess, I just don't know, it's just a bit boring.

Phil   It's the opposite of boring, you just haven't seen a great actor do it yet.

Nina   Have you seen Baz Luhrmann's *Romeo + Juliet*?

Phil   No.

Nina   I loved the concept.

What's the 'concept' for this production of *Henry V*?

Phil   It's really quite . . . Actually, I'll just show you. He sent me a picture of the model box the other day. This is great!

He shows **Nina** *a picture on his phone.*

Nina   Oh.

Phil   I know, right?

Nina   Well.

Phil   Catherine's a genius, always super bold. I've known her for ages, we used to go out, before she met Stuart.

Nina   Wow.

Phil   Yeah, I really thought we had something, but yeah, you don't get what isn't for you. That's what we say in this business.

Nina   What is this?

Phil   I don't know actually, it's a counter and . . . this is . . .

Nina   It's a kebab shop!

Phil   Oh, I guess, yeah.

Nina   It's a kebab shop with a load of St George's flags. That's his concept for *Henry V*?

Phil   Yeah interesting, I hadn't realised, he did say something about contemporary Britain – Wait, he sent a note in the email –

Nina   Don't you think it's a bit? All the flags? It's very National Front vibes.

Phil   What? No, I don't actually. That's a bit extreme.

Nina   There's just a lot of St George's flags that's all and it feels a bit dodgy to me.

Phil *now sees the design in a different light*.

Phil   Oh no see. He wants to set it in the future so, Europe has been taken over by the alt right fascists and the UK is like the last bastion of freedom and we're going to liberate France. Kind of like World War Two, so in the context of the production, the flags mean something quite different.

Nina   His concept is an English anti-fascist nationalist kebab shop reimagining of the Second World War set in the future?

Phil   That's just the backdrop; at it's core it's simply a coming of age story. Henry is a troubled young lost prince and suddenly his dad dies and he has to grow up and be this hero and . . .

Nina   And massacre people?

Phil   If that's what you want to see –

Nina   How could you see anything else?

Phil   How old are you?

Nina   What's that got to do with anything?

Phil   Sorry, I'm not trying to be patronising, I just, I like your energy, that conviction, it's refreshing.

Nina   Thanks . . . I like your energy too.

Phil   You've got that strong opposition.

Nina   Ha, thanks, but like, I'm open too! I mean it will be interesting what we do with that.

Phil   Definitely, after all, acting is doing.

Nina   That's what I always say, I hate plays where people are just standing around talking like, FUCKING DO SOMETHING.

Phil   Totally totally, ACTING, what are the ACTS?

Nina   Yeah, the events, what is actually happening between people.

Phil   Yeah, just do it, you DO the play you don't SPEAK the play, you speak a poem.

Nina   One hundred per cent, like, if there's no sound or if I speak another language I should still know what's going on.

Phil   YES YES YES. I'm with you.

Nina   Like, what are we doing now?

Phil   We're waiting for the stage management.

Nina   Great, let's fucking wait then.

They wait.

Phil   I know what you mean.

Beat.

About the flags. I get that sometimes. When I see a discarded mini flag on a toothpick, or when someone serves me a cup of tea in a mug with a flag or when the flag is hanging on a pole or a window, limp, tired, forgotten. How these, sometimes even cute symbols, have a way of entering our everyday lives, how they live in our routine. The way they make their ways into our bedrooms or into our recycling bins and if that's something that's difficult for you to see, to digest then it can be a shock. What to everyone else is security or perhaps just another random image, something people take for granted, no big deal, it's just a flag for god's sake . . . but to you, it's a danger, it's offensive, it's death. Now you're scared, now you're not safe, now you're thinking: am I gonna be OK here?

Beat.

Nina   Are you OK, Phil?

Phil   Yeah yeah, I am.

They wait.

Nina   Come on, let's fucking act.

Phil   OK, let's.

Nina   Like, we should be trying to get in.

Phil   Yes OK, let's fucking do it.

Nina   Let's break in.

Phil   What? Alright.

Phil *takes out a chainsaw from his bag.*

Nina   What the fuck?!

Phil   It's only a small one.

Nina   Is this allowed?

Phil *takes out other weapons – a drill, an axe, baseball bat, mallet and knives and more.*

Nina   Why do you have all of these weapons?

Phil   I'm a fight specialist. I was in *Band of Brothers*, this war series last year and got quite into it.

Nina   Oh yeah, I think my mum watched that. Were you a terrorist?

Phil   Yeah.

Nina   Do you get that a lot?

Phil   A bit. A lot.

Nina   That must be hard.

Phil   Why?

Nina   Well, it must take a toll, all that violence.

Phil   It's not real.

Nina   Yeah, but in your mind, you know your body can't tell the difference between real violence and fake violence.

Phil   Is that right?

Nina   Yeah.

Phil   I don't know, at the end of the day it's just a job. But I guess sometimes when the emails come through from my agent and it's another war thing . . . I think how many people am I going to have to shoot, or blow up, or maim, or stab, or drown this time? I guess I should be grateful for the work.

Nina   Come on! Fuck that, let's do this!

Phil   Right! Yeah! Come on!

Nina   We've got to take our destiny into our own hands!

Phil   Yeah!

Nina   Let's get into this fucking building.

Phil   YES!

Nina   OK, one, two, three
CHHHHAAAAARRRRRGGGGGEEEEEE.

They grab weapons and start battering the door.

They to break the door down but –

Sound of sirens, ambulance, police lights. Chaos.

They panic realising what this looks like from the outside.

Start scrambling to run away, hide.

Phil's *phone rings.*

Phil   Hello? Victoria, sorry we were late!!! The door . . . we got carried away, it was just a joke! Sorry. (*Listens.*) What?! Oh my god. What? Oh my god.

Nina   What is it?

Phil   It's Stuart! He had a stroke in the rehearsal room just now and . . . he's dead. Stuart Dunlop is dead.

Blackout.

Scene Two

The rehearsal

Nina *storms into the room in floods of tears, half in costume. Trying to hold it together, shuts the door behind her taking deep shaky breaths, obviously in a state of panic. She hurls herself in the corner crying, hiding, she is there for a few minutes.*

Knocking at the door.

Phil   Nina?! Nina?! Are you OK? That was out of order, please don't take it personally, can I come in? Will you let me in?

Nina   I'm fine. (*She's obviously not fine.*)

Phil   Martin is just upset about Stuart. I promise it's not about you. Everyone is just quite tense, because of all these accidents and they are taking it out on you.

Nina *goes to the door and lets* **Phil** *in. He gives her a hug.*

Phil   It's going to be OK!

Nina   I'm such a cry-baby, I know this is making it worse.

Phil   They're not really giving you a chance in there, if I'm honest, anyone would be finding it difficult without all of this going on.

Nina   I just don't know what's happening to me. I feel like I'm constantly doing all this work and then I get in the room in front of Martin and all those people who just hate that I'm not Stuart and I just freeze and forget.

Phil   It happens, it happens, can I offer something, might help.

Nina   Please do I'm so embarrassed,

Phil   You're really making this about you and you don't have to.

Nina   I'm so selfish.

Phil   No I don't, quite the opposite, but I think all this anxiety about whether you're good or not, the imposter syndrome, it's just holding you back.

Nina   No shit! Ugh fuck them. Sorry, but I just feel so. Trapped! Like some nightmare. It's just like I'm totally miscast. I feel like everyone's setting me up to fail! I'm going to quit. I can't let them win. They can get another Henry.

Phil   ENOUGH! Listen to me, enough of all this. You've got the part, you're Henry, tough. But that's that! The sooner you accept it the better. So many people would kill for that part and you've got it, and you're wasting all your energy worrying about these people. Fuck Stuart Dunlop (rest in peace). Fuck, Martin. He wants me to play the Chorus as a Syrian refugee, do I give a fuck? No! I'm here for the play!

Nina   Oh no, a Syrian refugee! I'm really sorry, Phil.

Phil   No, it's fine, I don't care. I really don't. Fuck 'em all, you taught me that on the first day of rehearsals.

Get over yourself and start making it about Henry.

Nina   I hate him.

Phil   This might help. When I first arrived in London from Turkey as a nineteen-year-old. I barely spoke English but I used to go through the *Time Out* magazine theatre listings and one by one cross off shows and see everything, absolutely everything. I'd often be late to the theatre and not understand a word. People laughed and I wasn't in on the joke but still I went. Then one night I ended up at the National Theatre watching the *Merchant of Venice* starring Henry Goodman as Shylock. Again, I didn't understand a word of it but when Henry came on it was as if my world had turned upside down. It was my dad, the way he moved, the musicality of his voice, his anger (I'd only just told my dad I wanted to be an actor and he was so angry with me) just like Shylock was angry with Jessica. And there was my dad on the National Theatre stage with all his bitterness, fury, lack of mercy, thirst for revenge, his pettiness, in all his misery he was there. That night I cried my heart out on the South Bank. So I wanted to tell you that, because you never know who will see you perform. It could be a little Black girl, or maybe, sorry, I meant mixed-race girl, or actually just a white . . . any girl, or boy, or any non-gender specific, like just any kid could be watching you perform. But also, sorry, it should be a little mixed-race Canadian-British girl and maybe any kid also.

Nina   That's beautiful, Phil, thank you. But I'm not Henry Goodman, I'm Nina Bowers and this is my only professional credit.

Phil   You don't have the 'experience'.

Nina   Do you think so?

Phil   You have been thrust in the middle of it.

Nina   I don't have a perspective, or a story like you have, a point of view or a worthy experience to bring to the part. And the technique also, I need more technique.

Phil   You've got to give it a go or you'll regret it forever. I think you can do it.

Nina   Why do you believe in me?

Phil   Well . . .

Nina   Sorry, maybe you don't, why would you?

Nina *sobs.* **Phil** *watches her for a moment.*

Phil   OK. Get up! One of your speeches. Let's start with breach.

Nina   What? Like right now? Here?

Phil   Yes, breach now.

Nina   What about tennis balls? Or Harfleur? Or Upon the king? Or band of brothers?

Phil   Why not breach?

Nina   It's just the most embarrassing one.

Phil   What do you mean?

Nina   It's just the most *ACTING* one, the most Kenneth Brannagh one. It comes out of nowhere and everyone's been waiting for it, and it carries this huge weight with it. It's impossible. How am I ever going to get them to buy it?

Phil   Look, you can let go of that right now. They're NOT going to buy it. I never buy this speech or even violence in the theatre, or war. Do you? All these posh fops in military fatigues stomping around, it's cringe. What do they know about war that they didn't learn from TV?

Nina   But how do I make it good? I feel like the whole play relies on me selling the war. I want them to feel something.

Phil   Really, don't worry about that, you have very little control in that regard. If they want to buy the war they'll buy the war. You just have to give them enough of a thrill, a moment of danger, a loud bang, an unexpected move, maybe they'll give you a gunshot or blood. Trust me, I've dedicated my whole career to it.

Nina   That's so sad.

Phil   Long may your closest brush with war be a production of *Henry V*!

Nina   Right, sorry.

Phil   Why are you apologising?

Nina   What you've been through.

Phil   I'm lost.

Nina   The war?

Phil   What war?

Nina   The war, wasn't, hasn't there been a war in Turkey?

Phil   Um, well I guess there have been wars around, and I mean everywhere there have been wars, but not in the way that you seem to mean. I'm not sure what you are referring to.

Do you mean like the situation with the Kurds?

Nina   Yeah, I think that's it.

Phil   Or is it that fake coup thing that happened, but that was nearly ten years ago?

Nina   Oh yeah . . . There was this podcast I listened to and argh, I think my ignorance is showing.

Phil   I've also been in so much stuff about war, maybe that's it.

Nina   True.

Pause.

Phil   All right, let's get into this, shall we?

Nina   Yeah OK, maybe I need to like to run around or something? Kind of get in my body, I don't know.

Phil   Yeah, sure, whatever gets you there.

Nina *starts running in circles around* **Phil**. *Over the following she gets faster and faster.*

Phil   You are Prince Hal, your dad suddenly dies and you are thrust into the role of king of England. You take it seriously and believe France is yours. Those lands belong to you from a long time ago and now you've crossed the Channel with a boat full of your men to claim your right. You are besieging the small town of Harfleur and it's tough. Your guys are exhausted so you have to rally them back and three, two, one GOOO!

Nina   Once more unto the breach dear friends once more

Or close the wall up with our English dead.

Phil   Follow the language, take in the rhythm. Di dam di dam di dam di dam di dam.

Nina *is out of breath. She's exhausted already. Coughing and retching.*

Nina   Can I just grab some water?

Phil   Woah yeah, take it easy –

Nina *grabs her water bottle and exits.*

Phil *picks up* **Nina**'*s script reads, paces.*

He gives the speech a go.

He wouldn't mind playing the part.

Phil
   Once more unto the breach, dear friends, once more;
   Or close the wall up with our English dead.
   In peace there's nothing so becomes a man
   As modest stillness and humility:
   But when the blast of war blows in our ears,
   Then imitate the action of the tiger;

Nina *enters. Awkward pause. Has she heard him?*

Phil   Shall we carry on?

Nina   I'm exhausted. I'm stuck.

Phil   OK, come on. Let's mess with it. You direct me.

Nina   What?

Phil   Might help you to get out of your head, step out and look in. I'd value your perspective as well.

Nina   OK. Sure.

Phil

> Now all the youth of England are on fire,
> And silken dalliance in the wardrobe lies:

Nina   Sorry to stop you there, Phil, it's so good . . . I know you're not trying to make this believable, but maybe just a little more urgency? Or gravitas, like the announcement of the Second World War on the radio, the whole country is fired up. Like a Covid announcement from back in the pandemic days. Do you know what I mean?

Phil   Yeah, yeah, OK:

> Now all the youth of England are on fire,
> And silken dalliance in the wardrobe lies:

Nina   Yeah. It's hard, isn't it, to invest in the word in England, 'cause we're English, but we're not English, it's quite sticky, complicated, you know, actually I'm sick of this word England.

Phil   It's the bloody flags again. I'm allergic to it.

Nina   Maybe we could use the substitution method? I saw it in a seventies film about the Royal Shakespeare Company, this is what they used to do. Substitute England with something more straightforward for you? Sometimes the simplest techniques are the most powerful ones. Change it for Turkey, for example? You know, you might be able to invest in that in a more direct way. Think of that.

Phil   OK.

> Now all the youth of England are on fire,

Nina   No. Just say Turkey instead of England. Just as an exercise. Go on. Yes, actually change it. Fuck it!

Phil
> Now all the youth of . . . Turkey are on fire,
> And silken dalliance in the wardrobe lies:
> They sell the pasture now to buy the horse,
> Following the mirror of all Christian kings,
> With winged heels, as English Mercuries.

Nina   How did that feel?

Phil   How did it feel? I don't know um, different, cool, I guess. How was it from the outside?

Nina   Yeah, fresh. Nice not to be talking about England for a change, but maybe, I don't know, maybe we should take one step further and replace Christian with . . . Muslim?

Phil   Jewish.

Nina   I mean Jewish, of course, so sorry, I knew that. Oh and maybe, in that case English Mercuries with . . . well, if they're maybe Jewish kings then . . . with Israel?

Phil   Israel?

Nina   You wouldn't have a Jewish king in Turkey, would you?

Beat.

Phil   No, no of course . . . no, it wouldn't be . . . I mean . . .

Nina   I'm sorry, did I say something wrong? Would that even be possible?

Phil   Not at all, no there's really very few Jews in Turkey and even if there were more it'd be impossible really.

Nina   Exactly, that's so sad. Right OK, let's go with Israel then.

Beat.

Phil   Now all the youth of (*Stops suddenly.*) Sorry just to clarify it's just that . . . I'm not actually Israeli.

Nina   Of course, I know that. Ah, I see the issue here. If it's gonna be a Turkish king you'd should be Muslim. But if you want to stick with Jewish then you'd go with Israel. Which would you rather?

Phil   I don't think I want to go with Israel.

Nina   Did I say something wrong? Did I? Oh my god, I'm so sorry.

Phil   No, it's fine. OK, I'll just do it. But just to make it clear that, with everything that's happening now, I really should make it clear that I am against the current situation in Israel or rather Palestine. What should really be Palestine! The war I mean, it's terrible . . .

Nina   Me too. Me too, of course. Let's just do it.

Phil   I don't personally support Israel.

Nina   Me too. This has nothing to do with that.

Phil   I think Palestinian liberation is paramount

Nina   Yeah, I totally agree. It's just about the speech.

Phil   Yeah, OK.

>   Now all the youth of Israel are on fire,
>   And silken dalliance in the wardrobe lies:
>   They sell the . . . desert now to buy the . . . camels,
>   Following the mirror of all Jewish kings,
>   With winged heels, as Israeli Mercuries.

Nina   How did that feel?

Phil   I'm not sure. Weird. I'm really not sure what we're doing here.

Nina   I heard it differently.

Phil   I was saying different words.

Nina   That's not what I mean, something changed.

Phil   Yeah, if I'm honest I do feel a bit uncomfortable.

Nina   Is that a bad thing?

Phil   Not necessarily, but I don't think it's necessarily a good thing.

Nina   Maybe what you're feeling is investment.

Phil   What?

Nina   You know great art happens in our stretch zone, there's your comfort zone, your risk zone and your stretch zone. In the stretch zone you have to bring yourself. Maybe what you are feeling is bringing yourself.

Phil   I don't know, this whole thing . . . is it working?

Nina   If I may, I've seen you with the company, how you are with Martin and the others and how you are with me, and it's two different people, I think what I saw when you did that bit of the speech just now was more of the real *you* and frankly it was more interesting that what I've seen you do before, 'cause you weren't putting on you little RADA grad mask. (*Laughs.*)

Phil   Excuse me?

Nina   Oh sorry, did I touch a nerve?

Phil   No.

Nina   Sorry.

Phil   It's fine.

Nina   You're kinda sensitive.

Phil   Maybe you're just a bit aggressive.

Nina   Maybe you shouldn't refer to women of colour as aggressive?

Beat.

Nina   Sorry I'm just a bit stressed out.

Phil   Maybe let's just go back to the speech.

Nina   Yeah, great.

> Once more unto the breach, dear friends, once more;
> Or close the wall up with our English dead.
> In peace there's nothing so becomes a man
> As modest stillness and humility:
> But when the blast of war blows in our ears,
> Then imitate the action of the tiger;
> Stiffen the sinews, summon up the blood,
> Disguise fair nature with hard-favour'd rage;
> Then lend the eye a terrible aspect;
> Let pry through the portage of the head
> Like the brass cannon; let the brow o'erwhelm it
> As fearfully as doth a galled rock
> O'erhang and jutty his confounded base,
> Swill'd with the wild and wasteful ocean.
> Now set the teeth and stretch the nostril wide,
> Hold hard the breath and bend up every spirit
> To his full height. On, on, you noblest English.

Silence.

Phil   Where did you train again?

Nina   Not RADA, why?

Beat.

Phil   You've got a chip on your shoulder about RADA.

Nina   RADA people are dickheads. They think they are better than everyone else.

Phil   That's not true.

Nina   It is true. You've all got it, that smugness, your special little club. You think you own it.

Phil   Own what?

Nina   Acting Shakespeare the industry. Especially the insecure ones like you.

Phil   This feels off –

Nina   'Hey man, so lovely to be working together. Oh I don't know, what I was talking about? Talking shit, yeah. How are the kids? Mine, yeah two now. Five and eight. Yeah yeah, we're still in that area.

Hey Janet, see you tomorrow.

All right, see you, buddy. Hey Sharon, I thought your reading was exquisite. Oh please, don't be silly now, you've totally got it. Of course I'd be happy to help you with the French lines.' Your little stamp of approval shutting everyone else out!

Nina *starts tearing up.*

Phil   Are you OK?

Nina   It's fine.

Phil   Did I hurt you or something?

Nina   What? No? Am I too blunt for you? Maybe it's a Canadian thing.

Phil   What is happening?

Nina   You think I'm a bad actor.

Phil   No I don't.

Nina   Why can't you just be yourself?

Phil   Why are you so upset?

Nina   I'm sad for you, I'm sick of your white passing, posh passing, performance, you're so amazing and you just spend all this energy licking everyone's shoes.

Phil   With respect I don't think you know me well enough to speak to me like that.

Nina   OH SORRY! Am I being unacceptable, god forbid someone is honest with you about yourself, god forbid anyone tries to actually be real with you. Let's just do the fucking speech:

Nina *grabs the script and starts to do the lines.*

Phil *grabs the script back from her.*

Phil   What is wrong with you?!

Nina   Give it back!

They fight over the script until it's all ripped up.

Phil   STOP it!

Nina   You STOP.

Phil   You think I don't know what I'm doing with those guys? How else do you think we're meant to survive in this industry? Come talk to me in ten years.

Nina   I'm not like you.

Phil   Oh yeah?

Nina   No I'm not. I'm not going to end up playing a stereotype of myself for the rest of my life.

Phil   Really?

Nina   No, obviously not! Look at me now, I'm HENRY V and you're some white guy's idea of a refugee telling my story, glorifying me. I bet you never had a part like this. No wonder you're jealous.

Phil   You have no idea what I've been through.

Nina   Ah very clear, isn't it? You're right, this is my chance, there are worse things to be than a bad actor, I could be a sell out like you!

Phil   Sell out! You're the sell out! One taste of a lead part and you're ready to go into battle for England. Where's the critical revolutionary minded person I met on the first day?

Nina   Surpassing you.

Phil *looks at* **Nina***, she's like a monster, he turns and leaves slamming the door behind him.*

Scene Three

The Game

Phil *walks back in.*

Phil   Let's get some air in.

Nina   Yeah let's play dodgeball.

They take out a box with colourful velcro balls and put on velcro vests. They get the audience to hit them with the balls.

Phil   Well done everyone. Round of applause for all of us.

Nina   Is everyone safely settled in? Great let's start.

Act Three

Scene One

The Show

It's the opening night of Henry V.

Nina *warming up, prepping, setting the stage for the show. St George's flags appear all over. It's ritualistic and moving. The acting in this act is noticeably more heightened and stylised than earlier in the piece.*

Nina

Upon the King! Let us our lives, our souls, our
debts, our careful wives, our children, and our sins,
lay on the King!
We must bear all. O hard condition,
Twin-born with greatness, subject to the breath
Of every fool whose sense no more can feel
But his own wringing. What infinite heart's ease
Must kings neglect that private men enjoy?
And what have kings that privates have not too,
Save ceremony, save general ceremony?
And what art thou, thou idol ceremony?
What kind of god art thou that suffer'st more
Of mortal griefs than do thy worshipers?
What are thy rents? What are thy comings-in?
O ceremony, show me but thy worth!
I am a king that find thee, and I know
'Tis not the balm, the scepter, and the ball,
The sword, the mace, the crown imperial,
The intertissued robe of gold and pearl,
No, not all these, thrice-gorgeous ceremony,
Not all these, laid in bed majestical,
Can sleep so soundly as the wretched slave.

Phil *enters here waiting holding the statement in his hand. Debating.*

Nina *ignores him but maybe also includes him as the slave of the speech.*

Nina

    Who, with a body filled and vacant mind,
    Gets him to rest, crammed with distressful bread;
    Never sees horrid night, the child of hell,
    The slave, a member of the country's peace,
    Enjoys it, but in gross brain little wots
    What watch the King keeps to maintain the peace,
    Whose hours the peasant best advantages.

What?

Phil   Nothing . . . it's a great speech.

Nina   Yeah, they're all great.

Phil   Great Britain.

Nina   What?

Phil   Nothing.

Nina   I used to hate it.

Phil   I know, you used to hate everything.

Nina   I didn't. I was just afraid.

Phil   Of what

Nina   Greatness.

Phil *laughs.*

Nina *wasn't joking.*

Phil *hovering, restless.*

Nina   We've got a show to put on.

Phil   I'm not doing the show.

Nina   What?

Phil   I'm not going out there.

Nina   But, you have to. Has something happened?

Phil   Yes, no. Yes, something's happened. I've written a statement. And I was thinking of stopping the show and reading it out, it's about us about this institution. About how we aren't their puppets. It's about war and violence and the negative history of this play and it's about how I'm not a Syrian refugee and I'm not a kebab shop owner. It's about how we are human beings and people are right now dying in wars and sea levels are rising and our governments are selling weapons and fuelling the pain.

Nina   You don't need to say that, the play is already saying that, and more, that's why we're doing the play.

Phil   You're not serious.

Nina   I'm dead serious.

Phil   Nina, what's happened to you?

Nina   Phil, listen, it's called acting.

Phil   Please just read it.

Nina   Don't you dare fuck this up for me.

Phil   Can't you see what they've done to you?

Nina *turns to the audience.*

Nina   We've made it, guys. I am blessed to have such an amazing company of actors supporting me through what was a very difficult period. People have questioned my right to be here and I thank you all you being there for me. I want to share a story with you that has helped me when things with the show got difficult. When I first arrived in London. I didn't know anything here. I used to go through the *Time Out* magazine theatre listings and see every show one after the other. Cross it off the list and go see it. And one night I ended up here watching Stuart perform Henry. Alongside people from all walks of life, including a monk, next to me. And when Mark came on stage I was mesmerised and

transported to another world. He wasn't speaking
Shakespeare or English, he communicated in a deeper, more
connected way. And I believe that's what we must do tonight.
We are fighting for a new England, a new inclusive England,
Stuart's England and my england. This is my country!

We few we happy few we band of brothers –

Phil Hold on, stop! You've stolen my story.

Nina No I haven't.

Phil Yes you have, you cannot know about the *Time Out*
listing, you're too young for it. You weren't even born then.

Nina This story belongs to everyone. Don't be such a victim.

Phil No it doesn't, it belongs to me.

Nina Phil, when will you realise, these things you call
stories, are just a costume, we are merely players, accept the
universe, no one really owns anything, we're better together.

Phil You've completely lost it, you've . . . become this . . .
this England!

Nina You've got it wrong, I'm not England, I'm changing
England, I am the king, I am the king, I am the king, I am
The King . . .

Whisper echoing, soundscape as we shift into the production of
Henry V.

The world of the stage, **Phil** *as the Chorus in a kebab shop apron,*
statement peeking out of his pocket. Sweating, nervous, hot under
the lights. Middle Eastern accent.

Nina *does animal work 'off stage'. It's startling and uncomfortable*
to watch her as she stalks around in the shadows like an English
lion, watching **Phil** *with her teeth bared.*

Phil
    O, for a muse of fire that would ascend
    The brightest heaven of invention!

A kingdom for a stage, princes to act,
And monarchs to behold the swelling scene!
Then should the warlike Harry, like himself,
Assume the port of Mars, and at his heels,
Leashed in like hounds, should famine, sword, and fire
Crouch for employment. But pardon, gentles all,
The flat unraisèd spirits that hath dared
On this unworthy scaffold to bring forth
So great an object. Can this cockpit hold
The vasty fields of France? Or may we cram
Within this wooden O the very casques
That did affright the air at Agincourt?
Suppose within the girdle of these walls
Are now confined two mighty monarchies,
Whose high uprearèd and abutting fronts
The perilous narrow ocean parts asunder.
Piece out our imperfections with your thoughts.
Into a thousand parts divide one man,
And make imaginary puissance
Think, when we talk of horses, that you see them
Printing their proud hoofs i' th' receiving earth,
For 'tis your thoughts that now must deck our
kings, Carry them here and there, jumping o'er times,
Turning th' accomplishment of many years
Into an hourglass; for the which supply,
Admit me chorus to this history,
Who, prologue-like . . . who . . . who

Nina *freezes! What is he doing?*

Phil *drops the accent.*

Phil   I want to say something. I've got something to say.

Nina *pulls him off the stage.*

Nina   What are you doing?

Phil   Nina – we can't do this. It is in our power to stop this show and the oppression we're suffering. You're the one who opened my eyes to it and look at you now.

Nina   We have to go back on, Phil. The show must go on.

Phil   NO! The revolution must go on.

Nina   Have you lost your mind?

Phil   They're using us, they're using our bodies, our voices and our experience to perpetuate forever their supremacy. It's absurd, you taught me this, you opened my eyes and now . . . the only real choice an actor has it to say NO. You still know that's the truth. Let's go out there and read it together.

He pulls her on the stage.

He takes the statement from his pocket. **Nina** *looks at the audience, pushes him out of the light. She's Henry now.*

Nina
Sure, we thank you.
My learned lord, we pray you to proceed
And justly and religiously unfold
Why the law Salique that they have in France
Or should, or should not, bar us in our claim.
May I in right and conscious make this claim?
To the territories of France!

Silence.

Nina   Phil!

MAY I IN RIGHT AND CONSCIOUS MAKE THIS CLAIM?

Phil
The sin upon my head, dread sovereign!

Nina
Tell you the Dauphin I am coming on,
To venge me as I may and to put forth
My rightful hand in a well-hallow'd cause.
So get you hence in peace; and tell the Dauphin
His jest will savour but of shallow wit,

When thousands weep more than did laugh at it.
Convey them with safe conduct. Fare you well.

Phil *is in the kebab shop now.* **Nina** *is a punter waiting for her kebab,
pumped up, half drunk, making late night laddish noise, aggressive.*

Phil

Now all the youth of England are on fire,
And silken dalliance in the wardrobe lies:
Now thrive the armourers, and honour's thought
Reigns solely in the breast of every man:
They sell the pasture now to buy the horse,
Following the mirror of all Christian kings,
With winged heels, as English Mercuries.
The French, advised by good intelligence
Of this most dreadful preparation,
Shake in their fear and with pale policy
Seek to divert the English purposes.
O England! France hath in thee found out
A nest of hollow bosoms, which he fills
With treacherous crowns; and three corrupted men,
Have, for the gilt of France, – O guilt indeed!
Confirm'd conspiracy with fearful France;
And by their hands this grace of kings must die,
If hell and treason hold their promises,
The sum is paid; the traitors are agreed;
The king is set from London; and the scene
Is now transported, gentles, to Southampton;
There is the playhouse now, there must you sit:
And thence to France shall we convey you safe,
And bring you back, charming the narrow seas
To give you gentle pass; for, if we may,
We'll not offend one stomach with our play.
But, till the king come forth, and not till then,
Unto Southampton do we shift our scene.

Nina

Now sits the wind fair, and we will aboard.
I doubt not that; since we are well persuaded

We carry not a heart with us from hence
That grows not in a fair consent with ours,
Nor leave not one behind that doth not wish
Success and conquest to attend on us.
And now to our French causes:
Who are the late commissioners?

Phil *reads from the statement.*

Phil   Ladies and gentlemen, this play.

Nina   I said
Who are the late commissioners?
Richard Earl of Cambridge, there is yours;
Why, how now!
What see you in those papers that you lose
So much complexion? Look ye, how they change!
Their cheeks are paper. Why, what read you there
That hath so cowarded and chased your blood
Out of appearance?

Phil   This Shakespeare play has often been used as a
propaganda piece for English supremacy and
warmongering. Despite this cast, today this continues with
more strength than ever before.

Nina *grabs a St George's flag tackles* **Phil** *to the ground. Through
the following speech she locks him in a bind with one flag and stuffs
the other in his mouth.*

Nina
See you, my princes, and my noble peers,
These English Monsters.
O, What shall I say to thee? cruel,
Ingrateful, savage and inhuman creature!
Thou that didst bear the key of all my counsels,
That knew'st the very bottom of my soul,
That almost mightst have coin'd me into gold,
Wouldst thou have practised on me for thy use,
May it be possible, that foreign hire
Could out of thee extract one spark of evil

That might annoy my finger? 'tis so strange,
That, though the truth of it stands off as gross
As black and white, my eye will scarcely see it.
But thou, 'gainst all proportion, didst bring in
Wonder to wait on treason and on murder:
And whatsoever cunning fiend it was
That wrought upon thee so preposterously
Hath got the voice in hell for excellence:
All other devils that suggest by treasons
Do botch and bungle up damnation
With patches, colours, and with forms being fetch'd
From glistering semblances of piety;
But he that temper'd thee bade thee stand up,
Gave thee no instance why thou shouldst do treason,
Unless to dub thee with the name of traitor.
If that same demon that hath gull'd thee thus
Should with his lion gait walk the whole world,
He might return to vasty Tartar back,
And tell the legions 'I can never win
A soul so easy as that Englishman's.'
I will weep for thee;
For this revolt of thine, methinks, is like
Another fall of man. Their faults are open:
Arrest them to the answer of the law;
And God acquit them of their practises!

She lets go. **Phil** *falls to the ground. He's retching, crying, traumatised.*

Nina   Phil, Phil? Are you OK? That was amazing!

Phil   What are you talking about? Why did you do that?

Nina   It was all there. Just like we rehearsed it, just like you told me.

Phil   We didn't rehearse that.

Nina   The substitution method.

Phil   You can't just use my trauma like that! You're totally mental,

Nina   MY MY MY ME ME ME. It's all always about you. Let me tell you a story about me for a change. It might help you understand. When I first moved back to London I was seventeen. I'd just gotten into one of the most prestigious schools in the country, a royal school. My dad took me round central London after my induction and I was overwhelmed by imposter syndrome, all the statues and columns and big famous buildings, those imposing West End theatres, Nelson's column, the stone lions. I felt sick. How was I ever going to find my place in all this? Like there'd been some terrible mistake. My dad said to me, we built this country, *we* did, *our* blood, *our* flesh, *our* enslaved ancestors lived and died creating this country. He told me never to feel like it wasn't mine. And now here I am playing an English king in *our* England. This might just be a play for you but it's my birth right. I'm doing this for my people and all they had to sacrifice. And if you continue to fuck it up, I'll kill you.

Beat.

Phil   You're still a slave, Nina.

Nina *slaps him.*

Beat, pain between them.

Phil   I wish you could see it.

Nina
What's he that wishes so?
No, my fair cousin:
If we are mark'd to die, we are enow
To do our country loss; and if to live,
The fewer men, the greater share of honour.

Phil
But if the cause be not good the king himself hath a heavy reckoning to make, when all the head and arms and legs

chopped off in battle shall join together at the latter day
and cry all. We died in such a place!

Nina

God's will! I pray thee, wish not one man more.
By Jove, I am not covetous for gold,
Nor care I who doth feed upon my cost;
But if it be a sin to covet honour,
I am the most offending soul alive.

Phil

Some swearing, some crying for a
surgeon, some upon their wives left poor behind
them, some upon the debts they owe, some upon their
children rawly left.

Nina

God's peace! I would not lose so great an honour
As one man more, methinks, would share from me
For the best hope I have. O, do not wish one more!
Rather proclaim it, Phil, through my host,
That he which hath no stomach to this fight,
Let him depart; his passport shall be made
And crowns for convoy put into his purse:
We would not die in that man's company
That fears his fellowship to die with us.

Phil

I am afeard there are few die
well that die in a battle; for how can they
charitably dispose of any thing, when blood is their
argument?

Nina

This day is called the feast of Crispian:
He that outlives this day, and comes safe home,
Will stand a tip-toe when the day is named,
And rouse him at the name of Crispian.
He that shall live this day, and see old age,
Will yearly on the vigil feast his neighbours,

And say 'To-morrow is Saint Crispian:'
Then will he strip his sleeve and show his scars.
And say 'These wounds I had on Crispin's day.'
Old men forget: yet all shall be forgot,
But he'll remember with advantages
What feats he did that day: then shall our names.
Familiar in his mouth as household words
Charles the King, Johnson and Sunak,
Patel and Bandenock, Starmer and Reeves,
Be in their flowing cups freshly remember'd.
This story shall the good man teach his son;

Phil
If these men do not die well, it
will be a black matter for the king that led them to
it; whom to disobey were against all proportion of
subjection.

Nina
And Crispin Crispian shall ne'er go by,
From this day to the ending of the world,
But we in it shall be remember'd;
We few, we happy few, we band of brothers;
For he to-day that sheds his blood with me
Shall be my brother –

Phil *tries to gag* **Nina** *with the flag.*

Phil   STOP STOP STOP.

Nina (*through the gag*)   What the fuck are you doing get off
get get off.

Phil   I can't let you do this. The only reason you're doing
this is because you think someone is going to put you in a tv
show. You don't give a fuck about theatre or shakespeare
you're just a validation war lord. You're a war lord. You're a
tyrant.

Nina   I'm a king, I'm a king. I'm a king, I'm the king of
England, I'm the king of the whole world, I'm a great great

great great ancestor of a great great empire from a long line of emperors and I want to take France and fuck the princess!!!

Phil   Me too me too me too.

Nina   No no no no no no, you're just the foreigner who tells my story my big manly story, about my big war and my little army and my amazing triumph /

Phil *stabs* **Nina**.

Nina   What the fuck, what the fuck did you just do? Phil. What the fuck.

To the audience. As **Nina** *is bleeding out, trying to recover. Throughout* **Phil**'*s speech* **Nina** *pulls herself toward* **Phil** *and grabs the knife.*

Phil   I am not a violent person. I'm a sensitive human being, with a complex and rich history and an independent spirit and a deep sense of community, and love, and I want to understand people, and be understood by people and see and be seen, that's why I do this job. But it's hard because no one, or very few people have a frame of reference for my experience, which may or may not affect their ability to empathise with me so I either give them everything, the context they need to love me, or I act like them so they think I'm part of the family and speak to them in their words, words that come from the cannon's mouth. But I won't do it anymore, I am not a human shield in your propaganda war. Shakespeare, and white supremacy are hand in glove, and until we see it there's no moving forward:

Nina *stabs* **Phil**.

Chaos.

They are both weak and bleeding, **Nina** *is trying to hold* **Phil** *and* **Phil**'*s trying to get away from* **Nina**. *They keep stabbing each other. In a desperate pathetic chase slipping around in blood.*

Nina   I'm sorry, Phil, I love you but I can't let you do this to the play, the play is so much bigger than us. This play is a play about climate change and war and people's lands, it's about the roles we have to play, how they are challenging and difficult, it's about duty and foreignness and love and loss and friendship and politics and law and food and culture and tea and biscuits and coffee and croissants and the South Bank and Dover and empire and the Windrush Generation and the post office scandal and betrayal and money and sports and tennis and Serena Williams and the pressure of being a successful person and PTSD, it's got trauma and nature and change and legacy and pain and making hard decisions, it's about our relationships with our fathers, and how we all just want to make them proud but they just hurt us and die and leave us with their immigrant dreams, it's about grief and queerness and coming of age and Lawrence Olivier and World War Two and World War Four and the cost of living, and drugs, and fashion and gloves, and safe sex and arranged marriage, and kebab and fish and chips and the boats and the Channel, it's Labour and Conservative, it's the ULEZ, what's happening in Ukraine and what's happening in Gaza, it's about stories telling, it's about home and identity and the internet and war the culture war and the Arab Spring and 9/11 and how theatre is struggling post-pandemic, it's live, it's about being alive and also being dead being just one of long list of the dead and being part of history.

Phil   Stop it! Tell her to stop it, please. It can't be possible, one play can't be about all those things.

Nina   But it is, it is the genius of Shakespeare and that is the power of acting, and being human and sharing space with one another in these uncertain times, that's why we do this. Let me tell you a story that might help. When I was seventeen I moved to London, and

Phil   You're completely irrational.

Nina   I went through the *Time Out* magazine.

Phil   STOP DOING THAT. Please stop her!

Nina   And I went to see every show

Phil   You're too young for that. You're too young for the *Time Out*.

Nina   and one day I saw Henry Goodman playing Shylock and he was just like my dad and I went to see him after the show and he followed me into the canteen and he stuffed a flag down my –

Phil   Shut up. Oh . . .

Nina   oh . . . oh . . . oh

Phil   oh for,

Nina   muse

Phil   Oh for a muse of fire . . .

They both die.

The End.

Printed in the USA
CPSIA information can be obtained
at www.ICGtesting.com
LVHW021534140624
783255LV00002B/355

9 781350 510852